VIKING
INSTAGRAM MARKETING

Chapter 1:

Introduction

Instagram is a powerful photo sharing app. When it comes to leveraging this social platform for business, it's all about visualizing your brand. While you can certainly post photos to any and all of your other social platforms, Instagram differentiates itself (even from Pinterest) with filters which empower absolutely anyone to turn their photos into engaging and brand-building works of art. When it comes to deciding which social platforms to add to your website, and post to regularly—Instagram certainly can't be ignored.

Instagram Is a Mobile App

One of the most noteworthy differences between Instagram and some of the other sites you might be considering for your brand or business, is that Instagram is a mobile app. While you can head to Instagram.com after you have created an account and perform limited functions, the majority of the functions must be used within the app. Downloading the app is free for both Android and Apple. If you are using Instagram for your business, set up your Facebook account first. Even if you are not yet active on Facebook, you will need to link your Instagram account to its parent company (Facebook) to transition it from a regular account to a business account.

Why Instagram? Check Out the Statistics Below

We know that you only have so much time in the day, so you might be in search of some quantifiable facts as to why Instagram is where you should be investing your time and resources. Here are some statistics that businesses across every industry simply can't ignore. Instagram has over 700 million active users (yup, you heard that right), 400 million of whom use the app every single day. 80% of these users are outside of the U.S. Over 80% of Instagram users follow and engage with multiple businesses, products, or services. Over 250 million Instagram users engage with the Instagram stories (paid advertising) each day which makes it a dream come true if paid ads are your focus. Users share over 95 million photos and videos each day. Most Instagrammers are between 18 to 29 years old. 38% of women use Instagram and 26% of men. Over 8 million registered businesses use Instagram. Over 120 million Instagrammers engage with brands directly after their Instagram engagement—visit their website or profile URL, direct message in Instagram, email, call, visit other social platforms, or get directions. By the end of 2017, 70% of brands will be on Instagram. Over 60% of users have learned about a new product, services, business, or brand after finding them on Instagram. Instagram posts with hashtags receive over 12% more likes, comments, tags, and shares. The average business or brand posts 5 times per week.

So, clearly Instagram is where you should be marketing, based on audience size, usage and engagement, and demographics – not to mention that every other business is marketing there, which should tell you something. Now that you know why you should be marketing there, it's time to talk about establishing your Instagram marketing goals.

Chapter 2
Establishing Your Goals

Establishing marketing goals is critical to the success of your Instagram marketing. Countless entrepreneurs and businesses have setup an Instagram presence, made a few posts, and then let it sit untouched for months or even years. This is usually due to a lack or absence of goals. So, before you even begin establishing any sort of Instagram presence or strategy, you need to establish clear marketing goals.

Your goals should be specific, measurable, and attainable. They can be long term, short term, or a mix of both. Deadlines and milestones can be helpful as well. "I want to increase my social following" would be an example of a bad goal that will likely result in your marketing efforts petering out after a while because there are no specific milestones. "I want to gain 1,000 likes by Christmas" is an example of a good goal. It's specific, measurable, and certainly attainable. Below are some examples of the various goal categories you might be interested in.

Traffic to Website (Sales, Leads, Content)

Probably one of the most popular goals of Instagram Marketing is to funnel your Instagram traffic back to your own web properties. After all, most businesses don't do business "on" Instagram. You're leveraging Instagram to obtain traffic and convert that Instagram traffic into brand-followers, leads, prospects, and customers. So maybe your goal is to get people to a landing page with a free offer where they can subscribe to your list and become a lead. Maybe they're being sent to a sales page or an eCommerce store. Maybe you just want to do some content marketing and send them to your blog. Whatever the case, the end goal for a lot of businesses will likely be bringing Instagram traffic AWAY from Instagram and over to their own web properties.

Social Following (aka Instagram as Autoresponder)

In this goal category, your aim is to build a large number of followers. The reason we also refer to this as "Instagram as Autoresponder" is because the main sought-after benefit here is to increase the number of people who will see your posts in their feeds. In this sense, your Instagram posts become similar to sending out email broadcasts via your autoresponder. If you grow a large enough community, this can be very beneficial and if your content is engaging enough to get a lot of traction in the form of likes, comments, and shares, you can significantly increase the range of your organic reach into people's feeds.

Passive Presence

Some businesses might have purely passive goals. Simply being present and discoverable inside Instagram is a benefit that has wider appeal and greater utility than you may think. In many cases, a company's Instagram presence might supersede or at least augment what was once the role of a blog, assuming most of your content can be conveyed in the form of or attached to images. When people come across this content of yours and look at your account can see some basic info about your brand or business and get some traffic to your website. This same approach can also be used for events, communities, and brands.

Brand Awareness

Another goal that's less thought about might be spreading brand awareness and recognition. If you're just starting out, there's a good chance your brand might be in need of a jumpstart. If nobody's ever heard of you, a great way to increase recognition is to simply create and share unique, helpful, or entertaining content and get your name, logo, and overall brand identity in front of as many people as possible as many times as possible. If this is your goal, you want to avoid being salesy in the beginning. Ensure you're focused almost entirely on posting helpful, relevant, or entertaining content.

Expand Existing Audiences

If you've already got an audience, your goal might be to make it bigger. This can be done via several social marketing methods. Sharing viral content, either curated or created yourself, can lead to a huge increase in your Instagram audience. Although creating your own viral content like that can be great, if you don't have the time or means to do so, you can simply leverage existing content that's already proven itself to be viral by curating/re-sharing it with your own comments or angle added to it. Also, a few humorous images and memes can't hurt either. Other ways to expand existing audiences can include contests, sweepstakes, and gamification. Assuming your offers/prizes are compelling enough, incentivized sharing can be very effective. Just ensure your methods are permitted by Instagram's Terms of Service.

Enhancing or Repairing Public Relations

Do you want to set your company apart in the public eye? Do you want to associate your brand with feelings of good will and community involvement? Was your business recently involved in a controversial incident that requires damage control?

It doesn't take a humiliating public catastrophe to make PR enhancement a good idea. This is a goal that any business can engage in. Non-sales related campaigns can include photos or videos that foster positive values and goodwill or even involvement in social movements (be careful not alienate half your prospects) and noble causes. Did your business recently donate to a charity, build a school in a third world country, serve food at a local pantry? These are all things to post about. These don't necessarily need to be about things that your business participated in. They can be content about general things like a heart-warming video about helping the poor or caring for the elderly. Special holidays like Christmas, Thanksgiving, or Mother's Day also present opportunities to leverage emotions, foster goodwill, and enhance your PR.

Market Research

A hugely beneficial goal of Instagram marketing is market research. If you're just starting your business or going down a new path, Instagram can be an excellent place to learn more about your audience and your market. This can be done in a structured way with things like surveys and questionnaires, or in a less structured way by simply engaging with your audience, commenting, asking questions, and so on. Also, lurking or conversing in Instagram areas or content related to your industry can teach you a ton about what your customers want and who they are. Beyond that, you can monitor your competitors' accounts and posts to see what their customers like and what they're complaining about so you can adjust your business accordingly. Creating your own account, posting, and engaging within it is another great way to get a constant stream of market/audience data flowing into your business. Ultimately, your goal should be to come up with one or two ideal customer avatars that you can then base your marketing and product development on.

All of the goals you've learned about in this section require some sort of presence on Instagram. Getting that presence started is what we're going to talk about next.

Chapter 3:
Getting Started on Instagram

If you are setting up all of your social media platforms at once, first check to see if your exact business name is available on the sites you wish to join. Ideally, you want your profile name of all accounts to be the same. If your business name is already taken, find a creative way to get closest to it. You could do this by utilizing underscores, or adding your location. For example, the fashion label Zuri's name was already taken on Instagram—so they used "ZuriKenya" as their Instagram name.

If you are setting up all of your social media platforms at once, set up Facebook before you set up Instagram. This will both automate the process of setting up your account after downloading the free Instagram app, but is also required to create a business account on Instagram. If you don't have Facebook, you can sign up using an email account.

To switch from a general account to a business account, head to "Settings" and select "Switch to Business Profile." This will ensure that you have access to in-depth post analytics.

Next, you want to navigate to the "Profile" tab (the person icon in the bottom right-hand corner of your mobile screen) and create a 150-character bio. Your bio should be short, sweet and to the point—and should leave enough room for you to add your website URL. If needed you can shorten your website URL, but it is best for branding to use your full website URL, unless it is too long. If not your website URL, a website landing opt-in page, which should definitely be shorted. You can shorten any URL for free by using https://bitly.com/. If you have the room, you can even add a few relevant emojis. For example, a florist could add a few flower emojis.

If you used Facebook to create your account, your current Facebook profile photo would instantly populate as your Instagram profile photo. Most businesses use their logo for their profile photo, but use a clear image that looks clean and crisp—even on a small smartphone screen.

Familiarizing Yourself with The Instagram App

Before you start posting, it is time to familiarize yourself with the Instagram app. The app is designed to be intuitive, and easy to post and use while on the go. Every time you open the app you will land on your "Home" page. Similar to a Facebook feed, it shows the recent posts of the people you follow.

At the bottom of your screen, you will see 5 icons. From left to right they are:

Home—the small house icon will instantly take you back to your Home page.

Search—the magnifying glass is the Search feature. Use to search for hashtags, usernames, locations, or topics. Type in what you are searching for, then narrow things down and perform research by using the features that populate after you type in your search term:

- "Top" is for the top profiles for your search term.
- "People" shows you accounts with that search term.
- "Tags" shows you the top hashtags that contain your search term.
- "Places" shows you the locations/check-ins with that search term.

Plus Sign—the square box with the plus icon in the center is where you will go to add a new post to your Instagram feed. When you click on it, you will instantly be routed to your device photo gallery. If the photo you require is elsewhere, click on the drop-down menu next to "Gallery" in the top left-hand corner. Then scroll down to find the location of the photo you wish to post.

Heart—the heart icon is where you go when you want to take a closer look at current activity. "Following" will show you the recent activity of the profiles and people you are following. For example, whom they have recently started following, and what posts they have recently liked. "You" shows you who recently started following you, who recently liked or commented on your posts, or which of your Facebook friends have recently joined Instagram.

Person—the person icon takes you back to your Profile page. Here you can edit your Profile, and scroll through your most recent posts. This also shows you what users will see when they visit your Profile page. In the top right-hand corner you will see your most recent notifications. Click on the 3 vertical dots to access your Settings and Support, to automatically invite contacts, and to create paid ads and promotions.

Familiarizing Yourself With Instgram.com

Instgram.com is significantly different than the Instagram mobile app. You cannot create a new account or add new posts—but you can search other accounts, engage with posts (like, comment, share), perform research, and access and edit your Profile. As a business, this may be your preferred method of research.

Chapter 4:

Instagram Content Best Practices

Now comes the fun part of adding a new photo or video to Instagram. If you have never used Instagram before, the filters are the part that really make this visually engaging photo sharing app stand out from the crowd.

To add a new photo, head to Instagram on your preferred mobile device. Click on the center "Plus" icon on the bottom of the page. You will instantly be routed to your device photo gallery. If the photo you require is elsewhere, click on the drop-down menu next to "Gallery" in the top left-hand corner. Then scroll down to find the location of the photo you wish to post, and click on "Next." This is where the fun begins!

First, you must decide what type of post you want to create. At the bottom of the photo, four icons will populate:

Icon #1—This semi-square can be used to resize your photo or image. While your image will automatically resize to this allows you to zoom in a bit.

Icon #2—the infinity icon prompts you to download the free Boomerang app, which allows you to record your own 3 to 60 second videos. However, you can also upload your own.

Icon #3—this icon allows you to create a collage, click on it to download the free app.

Icon #4—here is where you can opt to create a slider that shares multiple photos in one post, perfect for creating a visual storyboard. You can add up to 10 photos or videos to each post. However, one is sufficient.

Once you have selected the appropriate icon above, or if you just want to create a standard post, click on "Next" in the upper right-hand corner.

Filtering Your Image

Instagram filters are legendary. They are an easy and intuitive Photoshop-esq. method of branding your content and creating visual consistency. They are also an excellent way to transform a sub-par image, graphic, or quote card—into a brand-building image. That being said, the image must be quality to begin with.

Filter—in the bottom left-hand corner you can swipe across the many Instagram filters. Click on each, to determine which makes your image look its best. That being said, for branding and visual consistency, 60% of businesses use the same filter every time. Currently, the most popular filters are Clarendon, Gingham, and Juno/Lark.

Edit—the edit option allows you to do things like zoom in on your image, adjust the brightness, contrasts, tilt, sharpen, shade, shadow, and much more. Edit before you filter.

Once you have edited and filtered your post, click on "Next" in the upper righthand corner.

Prepping Your Post

Now it is time to type in a post caption. While your Profile limits you to just 150 characters, you can add multiple paragraphs to your post caption—but don't feel the need to. However, you must make sure that your post is engaging, relevant, and has proper spelling and grammar. Feel free to add a few relevant emojis. Whatever you do, you must add hashtags to target your post. Posts with at least one hashtag receive at least 12% more engagement—but businesses should aim for no less than 6 per post, and no more than 15 to 20. We will go into a bit more detail about hashtags in the next section.

Before you click on "Share", consider adding your specific location. This is something you should do if you are at a live event, or are targeting a geo-specific location. You can also tag other Instagram members. You can add a URL, but it will not be "clickable." Last but not least, decide if you want to post only to Instagram—or also to Facebook, Twitter, and Tumbler. As a business, we suggest being strategic about this, because you want to have a unique presence on Instagram. You want to give your followers a reason to engage with you on more than one social platform.

Click on "Share" when you are ready to post. A copy of your edited image will automatically be saved to your selected photo gallery if you want to access it for future use.

Hashtags

Twitter might have been the social media platform to make hashtags explode, but Instagram relies on hashtags to hyper-target how and where your posts show up automatically in a user's stream, search results, or when similar posts populate. In fact, if your Instagram posts aren't getting much in terms of engagement, likes, comments, and shares—you probably need to kick your hashtags up a notch. Here are some hashtag best practices:

- Always add at least 5 hashtags, but no more than 15 or 20.
- Don't use the same hashtags for every post.
- Variations of the same word or phrase, are not the same hashtag. For example, #food #foods #foodie #foodlover #foodisyourfriend #ineedfood #foodfinder,
- Misspelled but trending hashtags are ok. For example, #luv for "love."
- You can use SEO and industry keywords, but have fun with it.
- Use the search tool to research trending tags, tags your competitors are using, and for inspiration for your hashtag variations.
- Trending tags must be part of the equation, but don't omit lesser-used tags.

- Try to create a branded tag, such as #YourBusinessName.
- Don't go too off base, but create hashtags that are relevant to your post. For example, if you operate a coffee shop and your photo is of friends having coffee together—don't hesitate to add in a mix of coffee and food hashtags, but also things hashtags like #hangtime #BFF #workinglunch #coffeebreak.
- If you are a local business, use relevant location hashtags—but think outside the box. For example, not just your city and state, but maybe your county, local attractions, local university, city nicknames. Chicago could be #chitown, #windycity, #chicagoland, or #magmile.

As you can see, Instagram is a unique social platform where the goal is to capture your target audience's attention by appealing to them visually. If they like your post, they may follow or share. Then it is your job to maintain their attention, and entice them to convert.

Now as great as all of this info is, it's not going to be of any use to you or your business if you don't apply what you've learned. So, roll up your sleeves and get ready to execute the steps in the following battle plan...

Battle Plan

Step 1: Spend an hour brainstorming your Instagram marketing goals.

Step 2: Think about what kind of photo and video content is most useful for your business or niche and develop a content plan.

Step 3: Take 15 minutes to create and optimize an Instagram account in accordance with what you learned in this guide.

Step 4: Start uploading, posting and interacting in Instagram using the best practices described earlier.